Concise Guide to Good Policy

Concise Guide to Good Policy

Mick Ogrizek

Published by Mick Ogrizek
2020

First Edition: 2020
ISBN 978-0-244-86612-9

Published by:
Mick Ogrizek
PO Box 388, Bright, Victoria, Victoria 3741, Australia
http://www.lulu.com/spotlight/Mogbooks

Contents

Acknowledgements

I would like to thank those people that were instrumental in me learning the policy development craft. Most of my work experience (almost 25 years) was with Victoria Police doing research and operational policy development. I have a lot of people to thank there.

First, I would like to thank my first manager at Victoria Police, Peter Mac. I had no idea about policy development or anything else really when I came to Force Directives branch (later renamed to Corporate Policy) but he taught me that operational policy was primarily about supporting the work of frontline police (it only took me two years to work that one out!). That meant, policies and procedures (in the *Victoria Police Manual*) had to address the problem, be accessible, be concise, be practical, easy to understand, and support accountability. Things that in time I came to realise, apply to all good policy.

Secondly, I would like to thank my former colleagues at Victoria Police who taught me that policy development is about problem solving, challenging the status quo, and applying commonsense. But primarily they taught me that the process of policy development is a team effort; it involves sharing and challenging ideas, and that in fact it can be fun. Well, it was for me anyway. In particular, thanks to Caroline, Col, Jim, Carol, Captain America, Tim, Kevin, Eva, Ollie, Alex, Sara, Kate, Gary and Steve.

I would particularly like to thank those people who have kindly reviewed earlier drafts of the book and provided comments: Steve M. and Gary T. Of course, they bear no responsibility for the final product (or at least the bad parts!).

Finally, I would like to acknowledge use of the photo on the front cover, which is attributed to Alpha Stock Images. [1]

---

[1] License: Creative Commons 3 - CC BY-SA 3.0. Attribution: Alpha Stock Images – (http://alphastockimages.com). Original Author: Nick Youngson (http://www.nyphoto-graphic.com). Original Image: http://www.picpedia.org/highway-signs/p/policies.html.

Preface

There are many excellent books on policy development, [2] so why write this book?

The main reason is that I think there is a need for a concise (i.e. short), practical, step by step, introductory guide to policy development. Most of the current books take an academic approach to the subject and most focus on public policy. That is useful but I think there is also a need for a book that deals with the essential, practical issues relating to good policy development from the perspective of the practitioner (the person developing the policy). Basically, a user guide for practitioners. However, writing more generally on policy development is challenging because policy can range from a simple paragraph in an organisational manual to complex legislation. It covers a broad field. However, I think the same approach to policy development applies across the board.

As I mentioned, the book is aimed at those tasked with the job of developing policy, particularly those new to the world of policy development. A book that such people can pick up, read quickly and get an understanding of the basics. Accordingly, the book is written with this audience in mind. I refer to these people, in the book, as "policy developers"; the people actually assigned with the task of developing policies. Sometimes people unfamiliar with how to draft policies are assigned with the task with little information and support. Unfortunately, some people (particularly those without a background in policy development!) think that anyone can do policy. However, policy development does not just involve putting down something on paper, it can be quite complex. The major challenge of policy development is defining the scope of the policy, achieving a balance between what is desirable and what is possible, and then putting all this in writing in a logical and accessible way. That is why

---

[2] Amongst the best is *The Australian Policy Handbook* (by Althaus, Bridgman and Davis).

sometimes it is more of an art than a science. [3] Sometimes what goes into a policy depends on the "vibe of the thing". [4]

Another reason for this book is that I think many of the available books on policy development are not as accessible as they could be. In this book I have tried to use a less formal, more entertaining and easier to read style. I hope this assists in understanding the policy development process better. In some ways I have perhaps oversimplified things in this book or perhaps others have just over complicated things. The reader can make their own judgment on that.

Finally, I thought there was a need to document my thoughts and experience (over 30 years) in relation to police development, I like writing, and, anyway, I have nothing better to do with my time now that I am retired!

---

[3] Acknowledgement to John Stuart Mill.
[4] Acknowledgement to Denis Denuto from *The Castle* film.

Introduction

What is Policy?

Defining its Scope

Before addressing the issue of how to develop good policy, I need to define what I actually mean by "policy". Traditionally, policy has been defined as "a definite course of action adopted as expedient or from other considerations." [5] *The Australian Policy Handbook* regards policy as "...an authoritative choice, based on plausible hypotheses that can deliver required value-added objectives...". [6] Other writers have argued that policy is a complex concept which can be understood in different ways. [7] While that may be the case, for the purposes of the policy developer (those tasked with developing policy) there is a need to define the concept in order to know what they are supposed to be developing.

My definition is a bit more pointed: a policy is a position or view taken on a particular issue or matter issued by an authority. [8] For instance, the decision by a government to pay unemployment benefits is a policy. The policy being that unemployment benefits will be paid, in certain circumstances, to unemployed people by the government.

Most of the literature focuses on public policy, policy made by government. However, I believe the concept is broader than that. An essential element of a policy is that it is issued by someone who has authority in the area that is the subject of the policy, be it government or a non-government organisation (e.g. a company).

---

[5] *Macquarie Dictionary* (2017).
[6] Althaus, Bridgman, and Davis (2018), p.13.
[7] Cairney (2012), pp.23-26.
[8] Acknowledgement to Campbell (1997), p.1, for the basis of this definition.

But the definition I have outlined is only the starting point to understanding what policy is. Inherently, policies seek to impose or guide certain behavior. While policies can be aspirational, most policies are aimed at making people (those subject to the policy) do things. Therefore, that's what I am concerned with in this book. For instance, in the unemployment benefit example, the purpose of the policy is to pay unemployment benefits, but such a policy has no substance unless it contains details on eligibility criteria, application process, assessment process etc. The policy is concerned with how people apply for unemployment benefits and who gets paid them. That is, policy is about getting people to do things or at least help them to do things.

Aspirational Policies

Just a further word about aspirational policies. Aspirational policies are policies like vision statements, value statements, and corporate philosophies. While these policies seek to change and/or guide behavior, they are, generally, fundamentally different from policy in the sense I discuss in this book. Policy in my view involves seeking to actually change, or guide, specific behavior or actions as opposed to supporting certain types of general behaviour.

Policy vs Policy Instruments

A policy may simply be in someone's head or, more usually, written down in a policy instrument. Policy instruments are usually the method used to convey policy to those subject to it (the users or audience of the policy). A policy instrument is used as a vehicle to implement and disseminate the policy. When most people talk about "policy" they usually, mistakenly, are referring to the policy instrument.

Policy instruments, in my view, fall into three basic categories:

- Formal instruments – such as legislation, regulations, ministerial statements, manuals, reports, directives, procedures, instructions, and guidelines.
- Informal instruments – such as statements in emails, letters, websites, or even oral statements.
- Structural instruments – where behavior is directed through physical, environmental, process, or technological design. Examples are, town planning, or funding initiatives that support certain types of activities. [9]

However, in most cases, in some way, the policy instrument takes the written form. Therefore, in this book when I talk about policy instruments, I am referring to written policy instruments. Just to confuse things, I sometimes refer to policy and policy instrument interchangeably throughout the book as the two, obviously, are so closely interrelated.

Types of Policies

Introduction

Policy covers a broad spectrum. However, in my view, policy falls into two basic categories:

- High level policy.
- Operational policy.

High Level Policy

In this category of policy sits public policy as made directly by government that usually deals with social or economic issues at a high level. Such policies are usually set out in higher level policy instruments, such as legislation.

---

[9] For more information on structural regulation, see Frieberg (2017), pp.362-79.

Operational Policy

This category relates to policy at the operational level, at the "coal face". Often such policy is concerned with implementing high level policies. For instance, an operational policy would include policies and procedures outlining how immigrants apply for admission to Australia and instructions that apply to officers assessing such applications.

Policy vs Procedures

A related issue is that some writers make the distinction between policies and procedures [10] or only see policy as being high level policies. In their view, policy are the position statements and procedures the mechanism or instruments for implementing that policy. But I think that is too narrow a view. Policy can be implemented through a whole number of ways through a number of policy instruments, as I have outlined above, not just through procedures. I think it is more helpful to distinguish between policy (high level and operational) and policy instruments.

But more crucially, often procedures themselves contain or reflect policy positions and vice versa. For example, legislation usually includes both broad policy positions and specific procedures (usually in the form of regulations). Sometimes procedures may reflect or implement higher or more general policy principles and at other times they can contain policy themselves. This is particularly the case where there is no policy on a particular position or situation (i.e. a policy vacuum). More broadly, policy instruments may contain quite specific and prescriptive procedures that apply, sometimes in the absence of any clearly stated high level policy.

The approach I have discussed above, also addresses the view of some writers that policy is not made at the operational level. In my view, just about every decision made when implementing high

---

[10] Campbell (1997), pp.1-3.

level policy, at the operational level, involves a policy decision of some kind. [11] High level policy tends to be quite broad and therefore is not able to address all circumstances. Inevitably policy gaps emerge. Additionally, policy is often made at the operational level because issues are identified in the course of implementing or applying the high level policy. High level policy cannot address or anticipate all the scenarios that can arise at the operational level. That is, a policy vacuum emerges which has to be addressed at the operational level. Either way, I believe, policy is also developed at the operational level.

Therefore, in this book, when I discuss policy development, I am referring to both high level and operational policy. However, regardless of the distinction, the same policy development principles apply to both types of policies.

Policy vs Regulation

Just a brief word about regulation, which is an area I have studied and worked in. Before I go on, I should make it clear that I am talking about regulation and not regulations. Regulations are legislative instruments. Regulation is a broader concept.

Regulation has been defined in a number of ways and there is some contention about its scope. [12] Some writers, however, believe regulation involves some form of government action to make people do things. Arie Frieberg defines it is an arm of public policy. [13] I agree with this approach as from a practical point of view, most people would think that regulation involves some form of government intervention as it has most impact on peoples' day to day lives.

Therefore, there is significant overlap between regulation and policy. Many policy instruments are forms of regulation. The major

---

[11] In the regulatory field, this was the finding of Lipsky (1980) who found that public servants had to exercise discretion (i.e. make policy decisions) to make government policy effective on the ground.
[12] Baldwin and Cave (1999), pp.1-2; Frieberg (2017), pp.1-2.
[13] Frieberg (2017), p.2.

difference is that policy applies to both private and public activities, whereas, regulation (by some definitions) only applies to public (i.e. government) actions. For instance, a company may have internal policies binding on its employees. That generally would not be regarded as regulation by most definitions. That distinction is important because the principles outlined in this book apply to policy development by all organisations, both private organisations and government bodies.

What is Good Policy?

The main aim of the book is to support the development of "good" policy. But what actually is this good policy?

Good policy is policy that is effective. Policy that works. Policy that achieves its purpose. There are a number of key features that make policy effective. It is policy that is:

- on point – it addresses the issue or problem prompting the policy.
- informed – it is well researched and consulted on.
- comprehensive – it addresses all major issues and risks.
- practical – it works in practice, "on the ground".
- clear and accessible – it is easy to understand and to follow (from the audience or user perspective) and is readily available to those subject to the policy.

As you can see these features of good policy are concerned with addressing two major aspects of policy, the:

- policy problem.
- user needs.

These features of good policy are simply two sides of the same good policy coin.

Why Aim for Good Policy?

Why should we be concerned about making good policy? Good policy is, as I have said, effective policy. After all isn't that why policy is developed in the first place, to achieve something?

Not always. Sometimes policy is developed for the sake of having a policy; to be seen to be doing something. Sometimes policy is developed which sounds and looks good but has no substance. It is not effective, it's just words on paper. That's called bad policy or a policy failure. It occurs more often than you would think. Such policy is pointless, it is a waste of time and resources. Sometimes it can be harmful in that it can result in some unintended consequences.

The issue of policy failure is a bit contentious. Some regard policy failure as not delivering the policy instrument through an efficient process. Others regard policy failure as occurring when policies do not address the problem that prompted the policy in the first place. [14] Bob Hudson, in the UK context, has identified four factors that often lead to policy failure: [15]

- Overly optimistic expectations – under estimation of the time, costs and risks, and overestimation of benefits.
- Dispersed governance – misinterpretation or misapplication of the policy on the ground.
- Inadequate collaboration – policy development and implementation not integrated.
- Vagaries of the political cycle – lack of political support for long term policy change.

My view is that good policy (the opposite of policy failure) is policy that both follows a process (that promotes efficiency) and addresses the problem (that supports effectiveness). In fact, the two are closely linked, as we will see. We come back to the issue of policy failure in **Chapter 8**.

---

[14] For instance, see the study by Andrews (2018), p.20.
[15] Hudson (2019).

The Policy Cycle

Introduction

Most authoritative books on policy development accept that the adoption of the concept of a policy cycle is necessary to support good policy and minimise the chances of policy failure. [16] A policy cycle is simply a policy development process. Having a good process for the development of policy is vital to good policy. In the words of Matthew Lesh: [17]

> Good process does not guarantee good policy – but bad process has a much higher chance of producing lower quality, uniformed, and harmful policy outcomes.

Policy cycles outline the (chronological) steps or stages that need to be followed in order to develop good policy (or at least maximising the chances of developing good policy). That is, a process by which we get to targeted, informed, comprehensive, practical, clear and accessible policy. The concept of the policy cycle guides us through the stages that a policy must sequentially go through in its development. It takes us from concept (need for a policy) to the completed product (policy instrument) which addresses all relevant issues and risks.

Different writers have proposed different policy cycles or processes. For instance, in the United Kingdom the following checklist (they call it the policy test) has been proposed in relation to public policy issues: [18]

- Purpose – Are you absolutely clear what the Government wants to achieve? Do you have a very clear idea of the high

---

[16] Althaus, Bridgman, and Davis (2018), p. 49; Bekkers, Fenger, and Scholten (2017), p.12; Page (2000).

[17] Matthew Lesh (2019), p.3.

[18] UK Policy Profession Board (2013), p.16. See also the blog: https://quarterly.blog.gov.uk/2013/07/12/the-policy-tests-transforming-policy-in-the-department-for-education/

level outcomes and outputs that the Government would like to see?

- Role – Are you absolutely clear what the Government's role is? Is there definitely a problem here that can only be fixed through some form of Government intervention?
- Evidence – Are you confident that you are providing world-leading policy advice based on the very latest thinking?
- Creativity – Are you confident that you have explored the most radical and creative ideas available in this policy space...including doing nothing?
- Delivery – Are you confident that your preferred approach can be delivered?

Others talk about a business case approach to public policy development. [19]

However, fundamentally all these approaches are similar. They all agree that a logical, structured, process is required in order to develop effective (good) policy.

In this book I adopt the concept of a policy cycle as I believe that the policy cycle approach is best at providing practical and clear guidance to policy developers and therefore in achieving good policy. The core of the book is structured around my version of the policy cycle. The policy cycle which I have developed is illustrated below:

---

[19] Institute of Public Administration Australia (2012), pp.12-14.

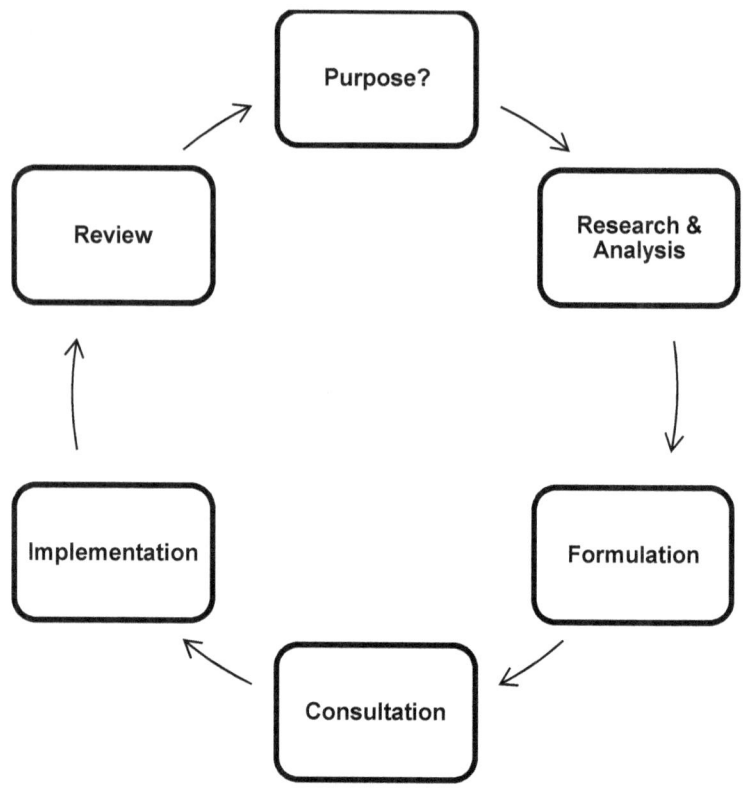

The process is a cycle because, in theory, policy goes through the process on a continuing basis, as part of the cycle involves a need to review the policy on a regular basis to assess whether it is still fit for purpose (see **Chapter 6**). So, after review, the cycle starts again.

How Long Does the Policy Cycle Take?

How long a policy takes to go through the policy cycle depends. It depends on how much time you have been given to develop the policy (there may be an urgent need), how complex the policy issue is, and how broad the application of the policy will be. In other words, the time needed should be proportionate to the complexity and risks associated with the policy.

However, if a policy takes too long to get developed it could become out of date. This could be due to a number of factors, the:

- need for and the basis of the policy could have changed (i.e. the purpose);
- evidence or facts underpinning the policy may have changed;
- political, economic, financial, or legal environment might have altered.

Application of the Policy Cycle

It should be mentioned that although, in the book, I talk about the development of policies from scratch (i.e. new policies), the policy cycle equally applies where you have been given the task of reviewing a current policy – the difference being your starting point being the Review stage (**Chapter 6**).

Limits of the Policy Cycle

Before I go any further, for the record, I need to make it clear that there a number of academics that believe that the policy cycle does not reflect how policy is developed in practice and that it is a simplification. [20] They are undoubtedly right. However, this book attempts to outline the process on how policy needs to be developed, to ensure we get good policy, from the perspective of the practitioner (the policy developer). There needs to be some sort of starting point for policy developers. For me, the best way of maximising our chances of achieving good policy (despite its flaws) is by following a process; the policy cycle. However, I am not completely naïve and I deal with the challenges relating to the policy cycle in a bit more detail in the last chapter (**Chapter 8**).

Another point I need to make is that the various stages in the policy cycle are not necessarily discreet and autonomous. While one

---

[20] For instance, see Cairney (2012), pp. 6-7.

stage informs the next, some overlap as well. For instance, implementation issues need to be identified at the Research & Analysis (**Chapter 2**) and Consultation (**Chapter 4**) stages as well as the actual Implementation stage (**Chapter 5**).

The Path Ahead

Each subsequent chapter (Chapters 1 though to 6) cover, sequentially, each of the six stages of the policy cycle. If you follow the process detailed in the cycle you will develop good policy. It's that simple! ☺

It should be mentioned that as each stage of the policy cycle informs the next, it is important for the stages to be followed in the sequence outlined, as far as possible.

Chapter 1: Purpose

Overview

The most important part of the policy cycle is of course the first stage: the need to determine what the purpose of the policy development task is. This is a vital part of the policy cycle as it determines the scope of the policy and what needs to be done in rest of the cycle. All good policy has a clear purpose. It is the foundation of good policy.

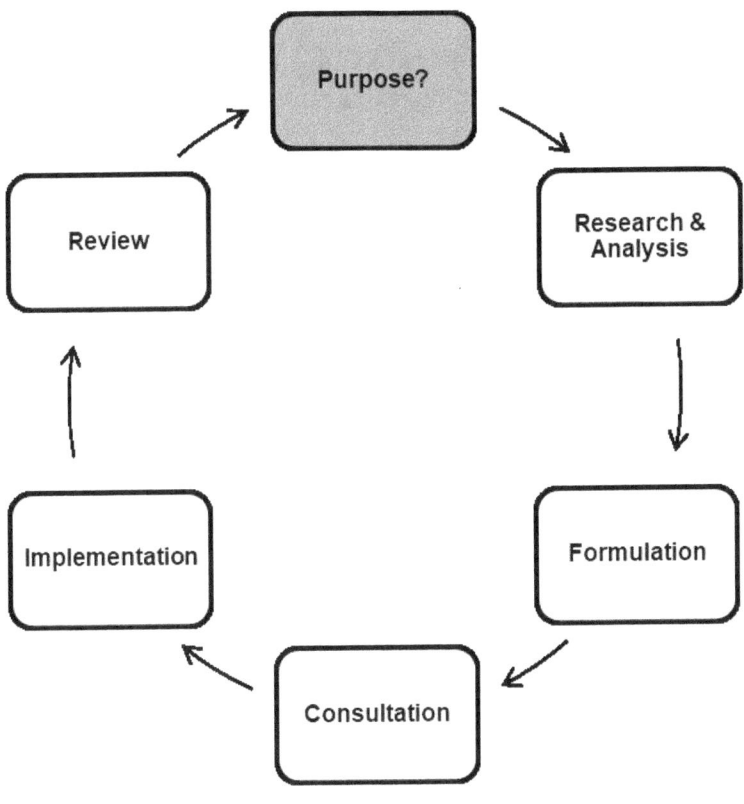

What is the Purpose of the Policy?

Often policy developers will be assigned the task of developing a policy on a subject because "we need a policy". That doesn't cut it as a purpose. A policy's purpose is what it is seeking to achieve. If all that is sought to be achieved is the production of a policy so the organisation is seen to be doing something, then that's easy. You don't need to bother with the rest of the policy cycle – just produce any old thing. This is bad policy.

I remember once when I was reviewing a particular policy. I was not clear what the purpose of the policy was and so I asked a supervisor in the field. His reply was "everyone knows". I indicated that I didn't know and that perhaps he could enlighten me further. He was unable to. That doesn't cut it as a purpose either.

Knowing what a policy is designed or intended to achieve is also important to determine whether it is effective, which is the essence of good policy (see the **Introduction**).

As mentioned, good policy has a real purpose. Usually, this means answering the question: what is the problem that the policy seeks to address? The main purpose of most policies is to solve a problem or problems. Most policy is initiated because a problem has been identified that needs addressing through policy. Its purpose is to solve a perceived problem or there may be a number of problems that need addressing.

How do You Determine the Purpose of the Policy?

If it is not clear from the paperwork (file, briefing note etc.) you have received with the task of developing the policy, you need to make further enquiries and ask someone in authority, i.e. your immediate supervisor. It is always preferable that you obtain details of the problem to be addressed by the policy in writing so that both you and everyone else (i.e. management) is clear on the scope of the policy development task you have been assigned.

Sometimes when you are developing policy based on another policy, such as implementing high level policy (for example, guidelines or procedures to support new legislation), the purpose of the policy can be gleaned from that high level policy.

When Policy is Not the Answer

Sometimes the development of a policy is proposed to address a particular problem but in fact policy can't address that problem or it is an inappropriate means to address the problem. For instance, a policy may be proposed because people are not complying with certain requirements set out in regulations. In this case, policy might not be the appropriate mechanism to address the problem if the requirements are clearly set out in the regulations. It may be an issue of awareness, comprehension, or accessibility. While policies may sometimes be used to reinforce obligations, there are usually other, better, responses to address the problem. For example, in this case, training, a publicity campaign, meetings or emails may be a better option as they might better target the problem.

At other times doing nothing may be a better option than developing a policy, considering all the costs and benefits of the policy. The costs and risks of developing and implementing a policy may outweigh the benefits of developing a policy response. The benefits of developing a policy may be so marginal or the problem so small, that there is little justification for a policy response. Often that may not be clear at this stage of the policy cycle but only emerges at the next, Research & Analysis, stage of the policy cycle (**Chapter 2**).

Planning

I am not generally a great one for formal, detailed, plans. However, for some policy developers plans are useful to provide some direction in the development of the policy. In the case of high risk or complex policy matters a plan is essential to assist in the efficient progression of the development of the policy. The plan should, particularly, identify any issues that require addressing, or require further examination, arising out of the identified purpose of the policy.

Conclusion

Before you can commence any further policy development you must be clear on what is meant to be achieved by the development of the policy. What is the problem that needs to be addressed by the policy? Only when you answer this fundamental question (what is the policy intended to do?) do you know the scope and focus of your policy development task. Without knowing that you can be going down the garden path or producing such a broad policy as to be meaningless or irrelevant. That's also bad policy. Once you know the problem intended to be addressed by the policy you are ready to go on to the next part of the policy cycle: researching the policy development task to give it some flesh.

Throughout the book (at the end of each chapter) I will use the immigration policy scenario to illustrate each stage of the policy process to hopefully better explain the points I have made in the chapter.

Scenario

You work for the Immigration Department policy area. The government has determined that it needs an immigration policy (in the scenario we assume there is no policy). That in itself is not enough information to inform policy development.

As a policy developer you need to know why the government needs a policy (i.e. the problem sought to be addressed). Is it because:

- Parts of the relevant legislation (high level policy) are unclear?
- The criteria that apply to immigration are too broad, unclear or ambiguous?
- A certain category of immigrants are applying to emigrate to Australia, however there is no policy on the criteria that applies to these types of immigrants?

Scenario

- Applicants for immigration are confused in relation to the application processes that apply?
- Departmental officers are interpreting the legislation in different ways when assessing applications?

It may be one or a number of these issues.

Chapter 2: Research & Analysis

Overview

There are two steps in this next stage of the policy cycle:

- Researching the subject of the policy.
- Analysing the results of that research.

This part of the policy cycle underpins an evidence based approach to policy development.

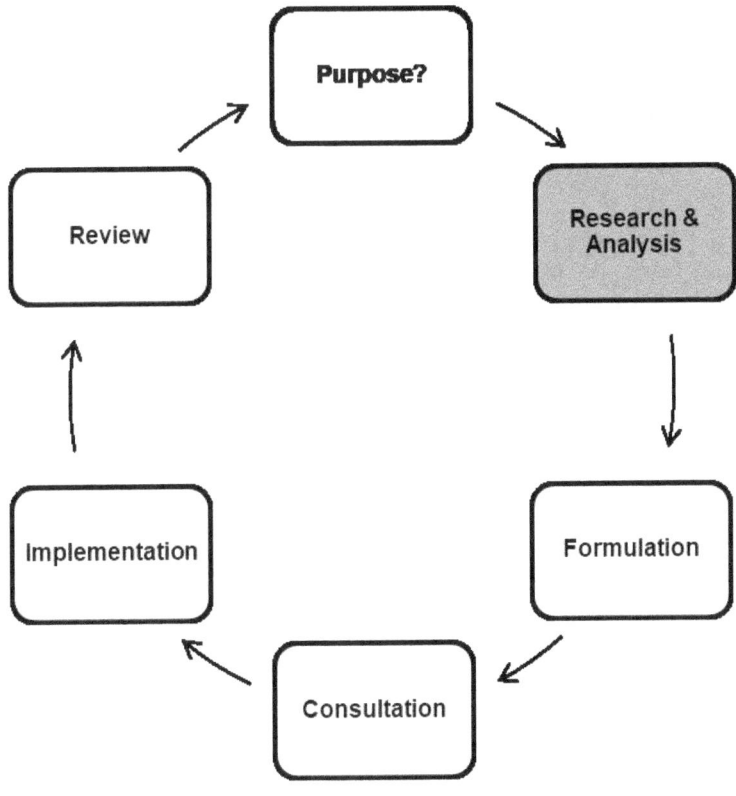

Research

Introduction

In the policy development context, research equates to taking an evidence based approach to developing policy. This is a term bandied about but it is essentially a straight forward concept: [21]

> …evidence-based policy (and practice) has been defined as an approach that 'helps people make well-informed decisions about policies, programmes and projects by putting the best available evidence from research at the heart of policy development and implementation' (Davies 2004, p.3).

As Gary Banks, has succinctly defined it, it is "…an approach to policy-making that makes systematic provision for evidence and analysis." [22]

What is Research?

Research is essentially gathering information (facts or evidence) in relation to the subject of the policy (what I refer to as the policy subject or task). The aim of research is to obtain information to inform the development of the policy; to give it content. Research assists in putting more meat on the policy bone; to inform the development of the policy.

Identifying the purpose of the policy task gives you a starting point for your research. The task of research is to identify all information related to the purpose of the policy.

A key part of research is identifying:

- Policy issues – these are key matters (the problem and any subsidiary matters) that the policy needs to address to make the policy relevant, comprehensive, logical, and work in practice (i.e. to make it effective). [23]

---

[21] Argyrous (2010), p.5.
[22] Banks (2018), p. 3. The term has also been more broadly applied to policy based on evidence, consultation, analysis, and debate, see the Per Capita (2019) report.
[23] See **Introduction** (What is Good Policy?) on what makes a policy effective.

- Implementation issues – one of the key issues that needs addressing or at least identifying, at this stage, is the costs of implementing the policy and who is going to pay for it, as well as any other issues involved in implementing the policy on the ground. Identifying these issues will inform the implementation stage of the policy cycle (**Chapter 5**).
- Risks – the policy needs to address any risks associated with the application or introduction of the policy. For instance, risks to employees; risks to the reputation of the organisation, financial risks, or any legal risks.

Types of Research

Where and how you obtain information to inform your policy can range from talking to people to conducting surveys. Research can simply be undertaking a literature view and consulting or it may involve adopting more complex methodologies involving qualitative and quantitative research. [24]

There are numerous research sources. Which ones you will use depends on the nature of the policy task and how much time you have.

Some suggested sources of research are:

- Documentation (file or brief) given to you with the policy task. Also look for other files on the subject your organisation might hold.
- Policies or reports (available on the internet, through libraries or by contacting relevant organisations for copies).
- Meetings or interviews with subject matter experts (within and outside [if appropriate] your organisation) and/or colleagues. Subject matter experts are persons, areas or organisations (in or outside your own organisation) that have specific knowledge of the subject of the policy. Subject

---

[24] See generally George Argyrous (2010).

matter experts include people who work in the area subject of the policy or who are or would be affected by it.
- Requesting expert advice. For instance, the subject of the policy may involve technical, financial, or legal issues and you should access appropriate, formal, advice, through your organisation. For example, seeking legal advice where the policy matter raises legal issues or risks.
- Books and journal articles.
- Authoritative and reputable websites (government or agency websites, news websites).
- Inviting public input. This could be by way of a discussion paper, terms of reference, or survey, on a web page, or meetings to gain input on the issues. This is usually only appropriate in relation to broad, high level, and/or complex policy areas and/or where input is appropriate from the public. [25]

By far the best sources of research are subject matter experts and the policies of other organisations. Subject matter experts are valuable because they cannot only provide you with expert, first hand, practical, insights on the policy subject but also direct you to other credible sources of information to aid your research. Colleagues (who have different backgrounds and knowledge), are also useful as they can put you on to useful research sources or contacts. Other, particularly similar, organisations' policies are also extremely valuable. They are a shortcut to identifying relevant issues and save you time. Why reinvent the wheel?

How Much Research is Enough?

Of course, that will depend on the complexity of the policy area you are researching and the time you have been allocated to develop

---

[25] A useful resource for providing guidance on engagement with the public is *The Australian Public Service Framework for Engagement and Participation* (www.industry.gov.au/data-and-publications/aps-framework-for-engagement-and-participation).

the policy. Ideally, you want to gather as much information as possible then you know the policy subject inside out. Your aim should be to become an expert on the subject – or as much as you can in the time you have available.

However, be careful not to chase every rabbit down every hole. When I was doing work experience at a legal firm, at the end of my time the partner asked me what I had learnt. I said that in researching and providing legal advice you can't address every possible issue or scenario. You only need to research the major issues and risks as you don't have the time to address every single possible scenario. I realised this after it occurred to me that I spent more time in the library than in the office.

Analysis

Overview

This stage of the policy development process is crucial. This analysis should be documented to assist you in formulating the policy in the next stage of the policy cycle (**Chapter 3**). After you have completed the research, you need to:

- gather the research information and identify all the issues and risks.
- critically assess the information.
- determine what the broad content and scope of the policy should be.

If any issues arise in this analysis, then you will need to do further research until you are satisfied you have a clear, comprehensive understanding of the policy subject.

Identify Issues & Risks

Identify and document all issues (policy and implementation) and risks associated with the policy issue (as detailed above, under *What is Research?*). You need to note all matters that you have identified, through your research, that need to be addressed by the policy.

Where the policy subject is broad and complex and you need further, broader, input to define the issues that need to be addressed by the policy, the development of an interim report or discussion paper may be appropriate. In these cases, the report or paper is circulated to management for further input. In many cases input may be also be necessary from stakeholders, or more broadly, to the public. This might have already been identified as necessary as part of the policy development process, otherwise consult with your supervisor as to whether this approach is appropriate before proceeding further.

Critically Assess

At this stage of the process, you need to critically assess the information you have compiled:

- Assess the information, including its logic and credibility. If several sources agree on an issue it is usually credible.
- Look at the material objectively, looking for any inconsistent or conflicting information. It is not unusual that information you obtain in your research may be conflicting, e.g. some subject matter experts or other sources of information may be biased or pushing their own agendas.
- Look for any gaps in the information.

Depending on this assessment you may need to do further research or consultation (e.g. with management, subject matter experts etc.) to clarify issues or fill any gaps.

Determine Policy Solution

You now need to determine what the content and scope of the policy should be, including what issues and risks the policy should address (document this to assist you in the next stage of the policy cycle).

It may also be useful to test the policy approach or approaches you favour (as there might be several options) by looking at its pros and cons. In more complex matters, undertaking a cost-benefit analysis may be useful. [26] In this context, you should consider whether there is a need for a policy response at all. The benefits of developing a policy may be so marginal or the problem so small, that there is little justification for a policy response. Dr Oliver Daddow has provided useful advice on this part of the process: [27]

> Do not seek the 'silver bullet' policy solution. Questions that should be uppermost in one's mind, therefore, are: Is our favoured solution worth it in terms of time and money? Is the policy deliverable? What are the risks and are they acceptable? Has the policy been tried before? Who will win and lose from the policy and what does this mean for its overall effectiveness?

If by this stage you don't have a clear view of what the policy needs to include or there are several policy options, consult with your immediate supervisor. In some cases, an options paper may be required to be compiled. This is simply a report to management/stakeholders outlining the issues in relation to the policy and major policy options (with pros and cons). The options paper approach is particularly useful if your research and analysis identifies some complex and/or competing high level issues or risks which are beyond your pay grade and you need input on the direction the policy should take.

Conclusion

This stage of the policy cycle is crucial as the research and analysis you do will directly determine the content, scope and approach of the policy. Whether you end up developing a good or bad policy will depend on your research and analysis. Therefore, your research

---

[26] There is a lot of literature on such analyses, which can be quite complex, a good starting point is the *Victorian Guide to Regulation*, Toolkit 2: Victorian Government (2016). Most proposed regulations are subject to a cost-benefit analysis in a regulatory impact statement. A recent example is the Victorian Children's Services Regulations 2020, see https://engage.vic.gov.au/childrens-services-regulations-2020.

[27] Daddow (2019), p.3.

and analysis need to be thorough as in the next stage of the process it gets serious: you get to put it all in writing.

Scenario
Continuing with the immigration policy scenario…you have determined that the main problem to be addressed by the policy is clarifying the legislative requirements that apply to the assessment of applications by departmental officers. You first need to research the issues: <ul><li>Look for any documentation or other relevant information within your organisation on the subject of processing applications (past or current).</li><li>Review the relevant legislation. What does the legislation (and any associated regulations) say about the assessment of applications?</li><li>Seek advice from officers (and their managers) involved in assessing applications to find out what they are doing now and what criteria they apply. It may not be appropriate to seek the input of external immigrant representatives or immigration agents at this stage of the process (but check with your immediate manager).</li><li>Seek legal advice on – <ul><li>the legal requirements applying to the assessment of applications.</li><li>any issues or ambiguities you have identified in the legislation regarding assessing applications (i.e. seeking clarification).</li><li>the current practice of officers.</li></ul></li><li>Examine the policies of other jurisdictions that have similar legislation.</li></ul>You then need to analyse the information obtained (as outlined above). In particular, you will need to reconcile the practice (what officers are doing in assessing applications) with what is actually required by the legislation, in light of the legal advice you have obtained. Following this you should be able to come to a clear view of what the policy needs to include. However, there still may be inconsistency in relation to what is legally required and its application in practice (i.e. by officers). In that case, if there are still unresolved issues, consult with your immediate supervisor, subject matter experts, and key stakeholders.

Chapter 3: Formulation

Overview

This part of the policy cycle involves actually formulating your policy:

- Selecting the policy instrument.
- Drafting (writing) the policy instrument.
- Reviewing the policy instrument.

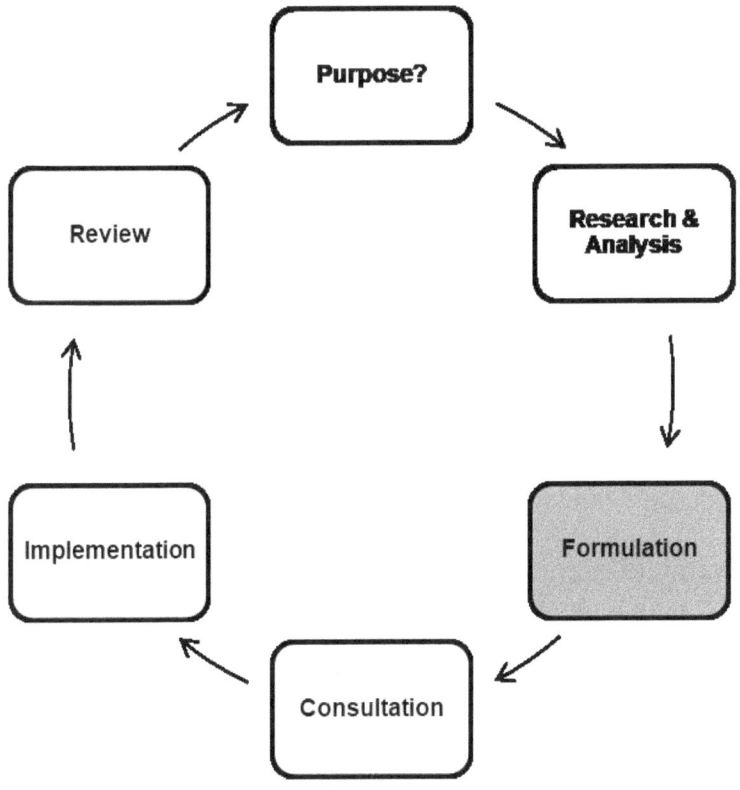

How to Select the Right Policy Instrument

In the **Introduction**, I briefly outlined the types of policy instruments that are available. [28] The issue of selecting the right policy instrument (sometimes called policy design) can be a complex matter because it goes to the issue of effectiveness. Which policy instrument will be most effective in achieving the policy outcome (addressing the issue or problem)? Initially, this means determining who:

- the audience of your policy instrument is;
- needs to know about the policy;
- will be subject to the policy.

A number of public policy writers have grappled with the issue of how to select the policy instrument. [29] An area that should be of interest to policy developers, relevant to policy instrument selection, is the concept of human centered design. This centres on the human characteristics of those subject to policies. [30] That is, how do you get those subject to the policy (the audience) to follow and comply with the policy? This approach has particularly been developed in the field of regulatory and behavioural studies which addresses the issue of the motivations of people. It is particularly, relevant in relation to high level policy issues. These studies give useful insights to policy developers when choosing the right policy instrument. As I mentioned it is a complex subject and if you have the time and inclination it is useful to look at some of these studies.[31]

Sometimes what policy instrument is to be used will have been predetermined for you as your organisation will only have available certain policy instruments. If you do have a choice of policy

---

[28] See the **Introduction** for the definition of "policy instrument".

[29] Althaus, Bridgman, and Davis (2018), p. 113-14; Bekkers, Fenger, and Scholten (2017), p. 143-51; Howlett (2014), pp.287-90.

[30] For instance, see Centre for Public Impact (2018).

[31] Some useful references are: Freiburg (2017), pp.198ff; Baldwin and Cave (1999), pp.34-34-62; Thaler and Sunstein (2009). Einfeld (2019) looks at the links between Nudge (an aspect of behavioral studies) and evidence based policy.

instrument, then you need to choose the most appropriate one by addressing the key requirements of good policy I have outlined previously. You need to ask the following questions:

- Which instrument is most appropriate? Which instrument is best at addressing the issue or problem prompting the policy?
- Which instrument will work best in practice? Will it work "on the ground"?
- Which instrument is most accessible? Which instrument is more likely to be accessed, read, and understood by the persons subject of the policy?
- Which instrument is most likely to be complied with by those subject to the policy? [32]

Sometimes one policy instrument may not be able to address all of these issues. Therefore, sometimes it is just a compromise. However, in some cases, it may be appropriate to use more than one policy instrument. Particularly, if you have different audiences who will be subject to the policy.

Drafting the Policy Instrument

Scope

There are a number of key things that the policy instrument needs to include:

- What is the purpose of the policy? That is, why is the policy necessary? Why is it needed and what it is trying to do? This is important for transparency, to get "buy in" from those subject to the policy, and to establish a measure against which the policy can be assessed for effectiveness in the future. [33]
- All major identified issues and risks are addressed. This is the substance of the policy instrument. The Research stage

---

[32] Particularly important in the case of high risk policies.
[33] As outlined in **Chapter 6**.

of the cycle should have identified what the policy instrument needed to cover. This part of the instrument includes all the requirements necessary to support the purpose of the policy. That is, what those subject to the policy or those administering it are required to do or follow.

- Designation of an area or person to answer and address queries in relation to the policy [34] This is important to assist in implementation of the policy and aid transparency. It is particularly important to assist in identifying any problems with the policy by inviting input.

Plain English

Introduction

All policy instruments should be based on Plain English or Plain Language principles. The reason why the Plain English approach should be used is to make the policy instrument as accessible and effective as possible. You need to communicate the policy message and Plain English has been accepted as the best approach to clearly communicate in the written form. Martin Cutts has explained the concept as follows: [35]

A communication is in plain language if its wording, structure, and design are so clear that the intended audience can easily find what they need, understand what they find, and use that information

I don't intend to get into the nitty gritty of Plain English as it is an extensive subject and there are a number of excellent books on the subject which cover the principles far more comprehensively than I can here. [36] It is recommended you buy one or more of these,

---

[34] Ideally a "policy owner" should be designated for each separate policy (or policy area) who has responsibility for managing queries about the policy and ensuring that the policy remains up to date.

[35] Quoted in Cutts (2013), p.xii.

[36] For instance, Cutts (1995). This is an excellent book and the book itself is a brilliant example of Plain English writing. I highly recommend it. This book has been updated and expanded by Cutts (2013). Also useful is the *Style Manual* (2002), which is the

and/or do a course, [37] to come to grips with the concept of Plain English. Writing in Plain English also takes practice.

Instead I will just cover a few key areas, with my take, particularly relevant to policy writing:

- Planning and layout.
- Content & Language.
- Format.

Planning & Layout

One principle of Plain English is to plan the structure of your instrument before you do anything. When I talk about "structure", I am referring to the ordering or organisation of the content in the policy instrument.

For me planning the structure of the policy instrument is worth spending considerable time on because it will make the writing task so much easier if you get it right (or close to getting it right). Your organisation probably already has a format for the policy instrument, so that's your starting point.

The process of developing the structure involves assembling the outcomes of your research and analysis (the policy solution) in some sort of logical order. You should have had this in your head (and documented it) after having performed the analysis of the research information in the previous stage of the cycle **(Chapter 2).**

There are two key requirements underpinning the structuring of policy instruments:

- User friendly – your audience are those people subject to the policy (i.e. those that are required to follow it), so it needs to be structured in such a way to make it accessible and easy to use by them.

Commonwealth Government style guide. Another great resource for writing in Plain English, although directed at lawyers, is: Macdonald and Clark-Dickson (2010).

[37] Some useful websites are: www.plainenglishfoundation.com; www.plainenglish.co.uk/services/training/courses-available/plain-english-course.html.

- Logical – this means grouping information that has logical connections together, then the document flows. Usually, this means following a chronological sequence (time order in which things are done). Having a logical structure is linked it to being user friendly: structure the policy instrument in a way that aids those applying the policy instrument in practice.

Your goal should be to make your policy effective (that's good policy), so you need to make it as easy as possible to follow and comply with. Structure is the first part of making the policy effective, the next stage is how you present and write the policy instrument.

Content & Language

One of the basic principles of Plain English is to use accessible language. That doesn't mean simple language. [38] Some key aspects of good policy writing are:

- Be clear and precise in your language. The policy will only be understood and complied with if your audience understands what you are on about.
- Cut the crap. Keep it short and concise by eliminating unnecessary content. As Chas Savage has said: "…ruthlessly discard junk. Junk is the text and ideas that are associated but not relevant to your purpose." [39] People don't have the time or patience to wade through a long document.
- Keep sentences short and to the point. One idea per sentence.
- Use words understood by the people that will read your policy and that respects your audience. Avoid jargon, archaic, legalese, sexist, pompous, arrogant, condescending, or flowery language. [40]

---

[38] Cutts (2013), p.xii.
[39] Savage (2019.
[40] See the following books for lists of words to avoid and alternatives: Cutts (2013), pp.24-33; Macdonald and Clark-Dickson (2010), pp.128-144.

- Write in the positive. Particularly, stay away from double negatives. They are only designed to confuse.
- Use a consistent style (e.g. format of numbers, names, titles of legislation etc.). [41]
- Check spelling and correct use of punctuation. Bad spelling and punctuation can easily undermine the credibility of policy instruments.

Format

A good format is more likely to engage the audience of the policy and make the content more readily accessible to them. Your organisation probably has a policy instrument template or format which you should follow. However, here are my suggestions for a good format:

- Use a font (typeface) that is easy to read. For instance, don't use one too small to read, or too many different types. For formal documents a serif font is preferred. Under no circumstances use the **Comic Sans** font.
- Use lots of headings to break up text and ideas.
- Use bullet points to list things. [42]
- Use tables to set out information more clearly (particularly complex, interrelated matters). [43]
- Include supplementary information in linked documents but avoid too many links or references to other sources.
- Minimise use of pictures, photos, logos, or charts. It's a policy document not a children's book.

---

[41] If your organisation doesn't have a style manual, the *Style Manual* (2002), is an excellent resource.
[42] As I have in this book.
[43] Martin Cutts (2013) has a useful chapter on alternatives to just words, see pp.178ff. An example of the extensive use of tables can be seen in my book: *Australian Childcare Regulation*, see **References** for details.

Reviewing the Policy Instrument

Once you have drafted the policy instrument, you need to review it to ensure that it:

- is consistent with Plain English principles.
- meets the criteria of good policy. That is the policy is:
  - on point – it addresses the issue or problem prompting the policy.
  - informed – it is well researched and consulted on.
  - is comprehensive – it addresses all major issues and risks. All issues and risks previously identified in the Research stage of the cycle are covered (i.e. make sure you haven't missed anything or inadvertently deleted something. Check back over your research notes).
  - practical – it works in practice, "on the ground".
  - clear and accessible – it is easy to understand and to follow (from the audience or user perspective) and is readily available to those subject to the policy.
- makes sense. Proof-read it several times.

The next step is to get others to review the policy. Submit it to your immediate supervisor, and maybe some colleagues and some trusted key subject matter experts for comment.

The whole process of review may require a few redrafts (remember to keep previous versions for audit purposes and to ensure you don't delete something inadvertently). Don't be frustrated or disappointed by this, that's part of the process to achieving good policy. All input should be welcomed (but not always adopted). The review process is designed to improve the final product. Getting the input of others gives an objective assessment of the policy instrument you have developed. As a policy developer it is too easy to be too close (and therefore possessive) of what you have produced. Remember the policy instrument must be able to be understood by the audience of the policy, not just you.

Conclusion

The writing of the policy instrument can take some time as you draft and redraft the document: refining the structure, clarifying content, getting additional information on aspects you are unsure of, and obtaining the appropriate input. This part of the policy cycle is an important part of the policy development process, you need to take the time to get the policy right, as far as you can.

Once you and your manager are happy with the final draft (and that's all it is at this stage), you can circulate or publish your draft for formal consultation, which is the next stage of the policy cycle.

Scenario

You have researched your immigration policy and are now in a position to formulate your policy.

Selecting the Policy Instrument

The first step is to select the most appropriate policy instrument. The main purpose of the policy is to address the problem of officers applying the legislation differently (see **Chapter 1**). Therefore, the main audience for the policy are departmental officers.

This would suggest an appropriate policy instrument would be an internal departmental document, such as a manual. However, in this case the policy subject is the legislative criteria that apply to the assessment of applications for immigration to Australia. This is an additional audience: potential immigrants. The policy, therefore, should be accessible to them too. The most obvious way to make such a policy available is by publishing it on the Immigration Department website. To avoid confusion and misapplication, it is not appropriate to create two separate policy instruments (one internal and one external to the organisation) which differ substantially in content. However, this does not mean that the two policy instruments must be exactly the same, the context and audience of the policy instrument will mean there will be differences.

Writing the Policy Instrument

The next step is to write the policy instrument based on Plain English principles. As your audience will be at least partly people whose second

---

Scenario

language is probably English, your policy needs to be in language accessible to those people as required by Plain English principles.

Reviewing the Policy Instrument

The final part of the process is to review the policy. In this case apart from getting your manager (and perhaps some colleagues and subject matter experts) to review it, it might be appropriate for a recent immigrant or somebody with experience in writing for such an audience to review it for comprehensibility (subject to management approval).

Chapter 4: Consultation

Overview

This stage of the policy cycle involves formally consulting with those affected by the policy before finalising it. Consultation is another part of the process that ensures more effective policies.

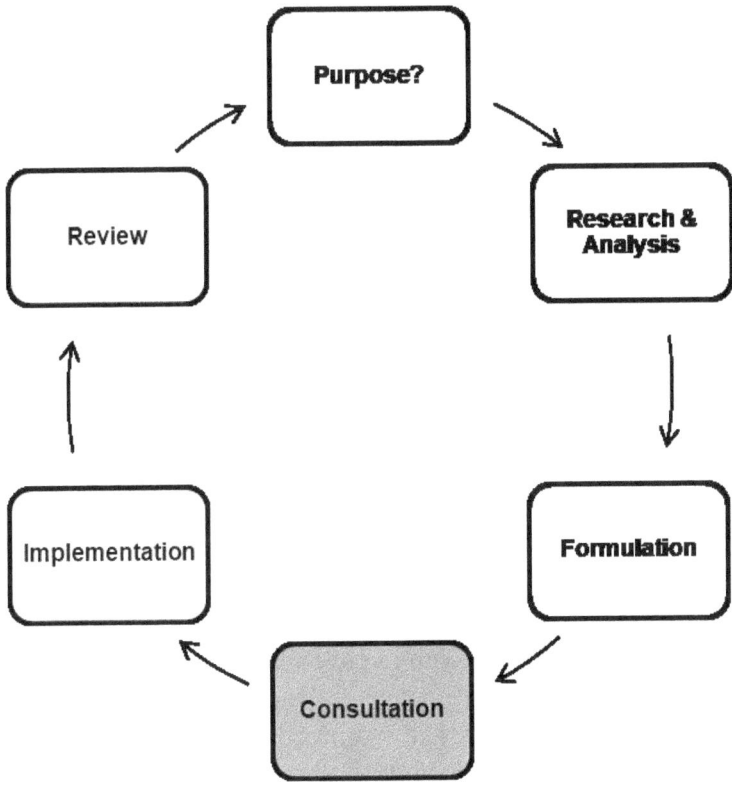

Why Consult?

In the early days of my involvement in policy development, I learnt the hard way about the importance of consultation. The organisation I worked for published a policy (which we were, internally, very happy with) only for it to be ripped to shreds once it got to those that had to follow the policy. From then on, I learnt to consult with people affected by new policies.

Consultation serves a number of purposes:

- Enables input to be obtained on the actual words of the policy instrument to ensure that the policy instrument reflects the purpose of the policy.
- Enables any unidentified issues or risks associated with the policy to be identified before publication and implementation. This results in better, effective policy.
- It's a means to test the policy to determine whether it meets users' needs. [44]
- Enables input to be obtained from people not consulted at the research stage of the policy cycle (see **Chapter 2**) who may have some insights into, or knowledge of, the policy issue.
- Assists in identifying any implementation issues associated with the introduction of the policy at an early stage (see **Chapter 5**).
- Validates or invalidates your understanding of the policy issues. You might have misunderstood or missed something (particularly if you are unfamiliar with the subject).
- Enables you to get "buy in" for the policy. If people have seen the policy before it is approved, and they are given an opportunity to comment on it, they are more likely to take notice of it, enforce and/or comply with it.

---

[44] This is the concept of user-centered policy design, see Moilanen (2019).

- It's a form of communicating or marketing the policy to those that will be subject to it, or required to administer it, before actual implementation.
- It protects your butt. It stops (or at least reduces the likelihood of) people attacking or criticising the policy when it is published as they have been given an opportunity to provide input, have seen you have gone through a proper and fair process, and that the policy has not simply been foistered on them. This is called transparency.

Who Do You Consult With?

This depends on your organisation's processes but I believe in as broad a consultation as possible. (given any time and other constraints). This is because, in my experience, the greater consultation you undertake the better chance that you will develop good policy and get buy in from those subject to the policy. Different people have different perspectives and this assists in testing the policy instrument before it is let loose in practice (i.e. published).

The extent of your consultation will depend on the nature and subject matter of the policy instrument. However, the minimum consultation that should occur is with subject matter experts and key stakeholders (including those responsible for enforcing or administering the policy). My view is that consultation should also occur with:

- All managers of administrative units within your organisation – whether the policy is relevant to their field of work or not, as you really don't know what insights they may have or how it affects their area. [45]
- Those people subject to or affected by the policy (including those that have to comply with it), i.e. subject matter experts,

[45] To facilitate the consultation process, it is useful to have personnel in each administrative unit or department that coordinate input on behalf of the unit/department. In my time with Victoria Police we introduced this role which we called Policy Liaison Officers.

stakeholders and in some cases, the public. In some cases it would be impractical to consult with them all (because of the nature of the audience) but it might be appropriate to consult with a representative sample or umbrella organisations (such as a union) or seek broad input via a web page.

For me, getting input from those actually impacted by policies is a vital part of the process as a policy that addresses all issues will be more effective. In some cases, this consultation may have occurred previously in the cycle (see **Chapter 2**).

Some people involved in developing policy are a bit hesitant in consulting too broadly. They appear to fear criticism or don't want any problems with the policy to be raised. But for the reasons I outline above, consultation is an essential part of the process; it's better for your policy to be criticised and picked to bits at the consultation stage of the policy cycle, than when it is published (when it is too late). Consultation also supports the principles of accountability and transparency. As a policy developer you must be prepared to stand behind your policy and consultation is the best form of scrutiny which keeps policy developers honest!

What Does Consultation Involve?

Consultation is simply the process of sending out the policy instrument and inviting comments on, or input into, the policy instrument.

It may involve, depending on the subject of the policy and its audience or your organisation's practice:

- Sending out the policy instrument for comment by the persons/areas you have identified, with a short report providing background to policy, including:
  - A summary of the policy. What the policy does.
  - Purpose of the policy. Why the policy is required. How it came about.
  - Research and consultation undertaken.

- Any issues or risks associated with the policy.
- The deadline for comments with the details of where comments should be sent; or
- Publishing the policy instrument on a webpage and seeking comment (including the background details mentioned above).

When Not to Consult

There might be circumstances where it might not be appropriate to consult on the policy instrument or at least to only undertake very limited consultation:

- Where it involves a sensitive or contentious subject. This is where there may be sensitivity on political, economic, financial, safety, or security grounds.
- There is an urgent need for the policy to be issued as there is no time to consult or there are large risks with delaying implementation.

Where it is a sensitive subject and some consultation is deemed necessary, it is suggested that a consultation plan be developed, with approval of senior management, then you have organisational support for your (limited) consultation. Sensitive policy issues can also be managed by having a working group consisting of management, policy developers, and subject matter experts responsible for developing the policy from start to finish subject to confidentiality requirements.

What do You Do with the Results of Consultation?

Once you have obtained all the comments on the policy instrument, your next steps are:

- Compile all the input. Setting this information out in a table or matrix may assist in managing the input obtained from consultation.

- Assess the validity of the input. This will usually require consultation with your supervisor and relevant subject matter experts/stakeholders. Remember to give feedback to those that have provided comments or suggestions.
- Incorporate the accepted comments in the policy instrument and produce a final draft of the policy.

All the above information should then be compiled in a summary report (see **Chapter 5**). Conclusion

Once you have finalised the policy instrument and compiled a summary report the policy instrument is ready to go to the implementation stage of the policy cycle.

Scenario

Your policy has now been drafted and is ready for consultation. It is suggested that the draft immigration policy, with explanatory report, (as outlined above) be submitted for comment to a number of areas:

- Subject matter experts – this would be the area(s) within the immigration department responsible for managing the policy as well as the legal department given the legislative issues involved.
- Internal stakeholders – this would mean getting the input of –
  - departmental officers who have responsibility for assessing applications.
  - embassies, consulates and any other areas involved in immigration applications.
  - all other administrative units within the Immigration Department.
- External stakeholders – getting input from immigrant and community representative groups, and immigration agents (subject to appropriate management approval as to how and with whom such consultation should take place).

Given the potential sensitivity of such a subject a consultation plan may need to be developed with senior departmental managers before proceeding with consultation.

Chapter 5: Implementation

Overview

The implementation stage of the policy cycle includes a number of components:

- Getting final approval for the policy.
- Coordinating implementation.
- Publishing the policy instrument and marketing the policy.

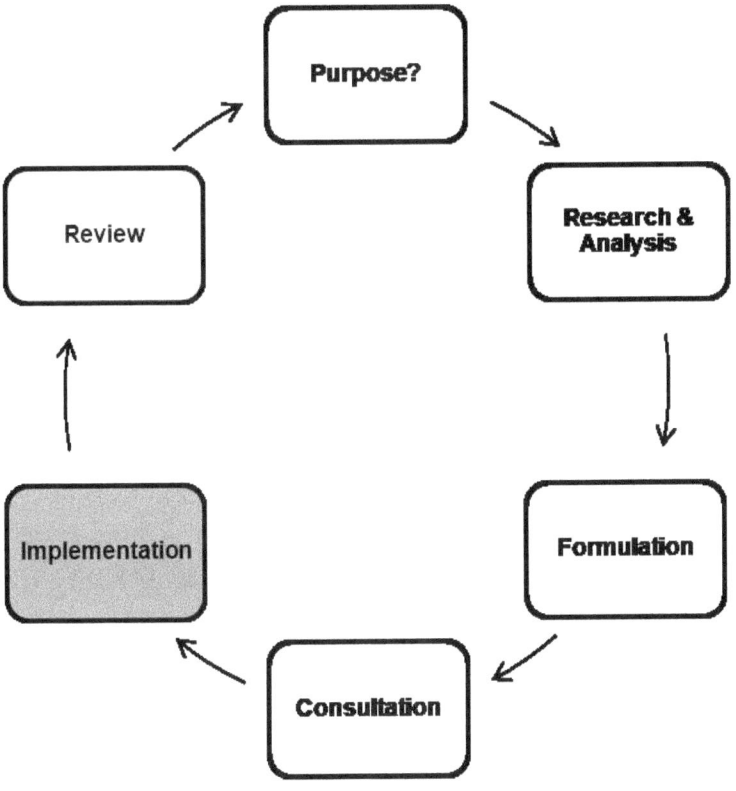

Final Approval

Getting final approval to the policy at the appropriate level is important to ensure that it has legal force and/or appropriate authority.

Within your organisation there will normally be a process to get sign off/approval to the policy instrument at the appropriate level. That is, by the person or area that legally (e.g. delegate) or by policy has responsibility, on behalf of the organization, to approve all policies before they can be published.

The usual process would be for the policy and a supporting report to be submitted through line management to the person/area authorised to approve policies. The supporting report should include the following information:

- Purpose of the policy.
- Summary of the effect of the policy.
- Research and consultation undertaken. Including issues identified during the formal consultation process and what action was taken in relation to that input (attach copies of the input).
- Details of any issues or risks associated with the policy.
- Details of any implementation requirements or issues identified (see below).
- Request for approval to publish the policy.

Coordinating Implementation

Once approval (formally and in writing) is obtained from the appropriate person in the organisation, you need to coordinate with other areas in the organisation to implement the policy. This must occur before publication of the policy instrument.

Coordinating implementation involves:

- Determining who will be responsible for implementation and the costs of implementation – this includes both the costs of the policy implementation process itself and the costs of the policy in practice.

- Choosing a date and developing a timeline for implementation – this would usually coincide with any schedule that exists for publishing policy instruments or other timeline, e.g. implementation date of new legislation. The implementation date may be a date specified in the policy instrument or the date of publication of the policy instrument. In either case, the date of effect of the policy must be clear.
- Liaising and coordinating with areas that are to administer or enforce the policy – this is to ensure they are aware of the date of implementation and are in a position to support its introduction. If they are not going to be ready by the proposed implementation date, you may need to change the date (in consultation with your immediate supervisor).
- Addressing any other additional, consequential implementation issues – for instance, forms or processes may need to be changed, training may need to be conducted, or other organisations may need to be advised.

It would be useful to develop an implementation plan (if you haven't already), including the information above and that is a checklist of implementation issues to be addressed (and their related timelines) before publication of the policy instrument.

Publishing the Policy

This is probably the most important part of implementation as by publishing, the policy actually comes into effect. People are then required to comply with it.

Your organisation will have requirements for the publication of policies. The type of policy instrument will dictate where and how it is published.

Marketing the Policy

Purpose of Marketing

Marketing of the policy should occur in parallel with publication. Marketing should occur at the same time or shortly after the policy is published.

Essentially the goal of marketing is to:

- Publicise the issuing of the policy. Simply publishing may not be enough for it to come to the attention of those people subject to the policy or those that need to know about it.
- Explain the purpose behind the policy. This is important to get "buy in" from those required to comply with it. It has been established if people understand the purpose of the policy (i.e. why it is necessary), they are more likely to comply with it or at least be less critical of it.

Essentially, then, marketing the policy is about making it more effective.

How do You Market the Policy?

Your organisation's public relations area can assist. It is suggested that a marketing plan be developed. [46] Marketing of the policy needs to be directed to the policy's audience (those subject to the policy or those administering it).

How you market the policy will be determined by the nature of your audience. There are a number of keyways to market the policy, the details of the policy, and the purpose of it (marketing needs to focus on all of these):

- Publication on your organisation's website and/or intranet.
- Articles in your organisation's publication (e.g. magazine, journal, or newsletter).
- Media releases.

---

[46] This can be part of the implementation plan (see above).

- Emails to those subject to the policy.
- Production of information sheets or leaflets.
- Holding briefings or meetings specifically about the policy.
- Attending meetings or conferences to explain the policy to relevant stakeholders.

In all these forms of marketing it is important to designate a person or area responsible for answering and addressing queries in relation to the policy instrument (the policy instrument should have designated the person or area to perform this function).

Conclusion

Now that the policy has been implemented your job is done. All you have to do is to sit back and wait for the accolades. ☺ Unfortunately, it doesn't stop there as an essential part of the policy cycle is to review or evaluate the effectiveness of the policy (including getting input on the policy), which is up next.

Scenario

Once you have prepared a report, providing background to the policy and summarising your consultation on the policy, you are ready to obtain approval to publish it.

Final Approval

The policy needs to be submitted to the appropriate level in your department for final approval. Someone in the Immigration Department probably has delegated authority to perform this role.

Coordinating Implementation

This is an important part of the process in the case of our immigration policy as it substantially affects the work of departmental officers. A few things that may need to be addressed are:

- Advising departmental officers assessing applications, embassies and consulates, of the date the policy will be published and obtaining their advice as to any implementation issues. It may be necessary to coordinate training of departmental officers administering the new policy.

Scenario

- Reviewing and revising application forms, information for applicants, websites etc.

Publishing the Policy

The policy needs to be published (as discussed earlier) on the Immigration Department website and departmental manual.

Marketing the Policy

In conjunction with publication of the policy there will be a need to publicise the policy through:

- Issue of a media release (given the potential importance of the policy).
- Producing information sheets or handouts on the new policy for external stakeholders.
- Holding meetings with external stakeholders (immigrant community representatives and immigrant agents) explaining the policy.
- Publication of articles in internal departmental communications publicising the policy and how it changes things.

Chapter 6: Review

Overview

There are two aspects to this stage of the policy cycle:
- Initial feedback
- Review of the policy.

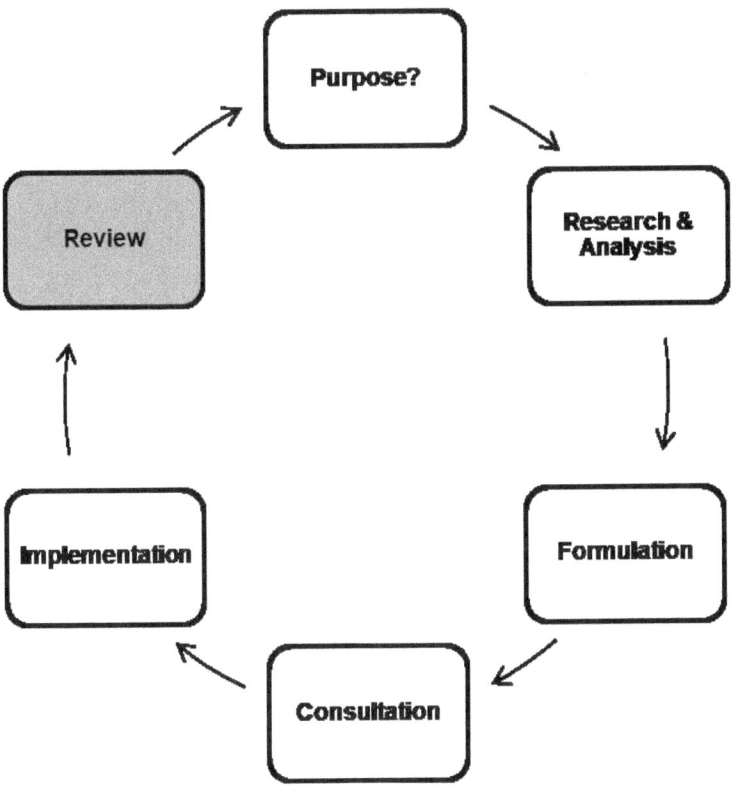

Initial Feedback

Once the policy instrument is published, undoubtedly, you will get feedback on the policy. This feedback might come directly (to the policy developer) or through the subject matter expert responsible for the policy (see **Chapter 5**). Rarely is this congratulating you on a great job (see **Chapter 8**). Sometimes this feedback is simply based on the fact that the person/area doesn't like the policy. You can address that by communicating with them and explaining the situation.

However, it is possible that legitimate issues are raised. For instance, where there is an ambiguity in the policy or there is something that might have been missed. You can address these issues by issuing an email (or another appropriate means of communication) clarifying the policy, or alternatively (which will take much longer) amending the policy. This action is of course done in conjunction with your immediate supervisor. The policy should only be amended and reissued if there is a major problem with the policy.

Reviews

Why Review Policies?

Policies need to be reviewed frequently as the environment (political, economic, financial, legal, social), level of knowledge and priorities change. Policies are constantly evolving and developing to keep up with these changes. If policies don't keep up with these changes they quickly become out of date and are no longer effective. They become bad policy very quickly (see **Introduction**).

The process of policy review is also a process of "continuous improvement" where you are, on an ongoing basis, assessing what you have done and from that, improving on it. I have only ever come across what I thought was a perfect policy once in my career (I didn't write it). It has been revised about four times in about seven years since it was first issued. Even the best policies need regular review; it's an important part of the policy cycle. More broadly, reviewing policies is important for learning. You can learn from what has not worked (policy failures) and what has worked. The only way to know this is by reviewing policies. That's why this part of the cycle is important.

Unfortunately, the importance of the task of reviewing policies is underrated and is often overlooked. In many organisations, it is not regarded as important as other parts of the cycle. Once the policy is published there is usually little interest in revisiting it until something goes wrong. However, it is far better to be proactive and to identify and address any issues before something goes wrong when there is panic to fix the problem. Which usually results in some ad hoc, band aid solution (i.e. bad policy).

How Often Should Reviews be Undertaken?

Reviews of policy should be conducted on a regular basis. It is suggested policies be reviewed one or two years after publication. High risk policies may need to be reviewed more regularly.

Some policy instruments have inbuilt periods for review or organisations may have a schedule for review of policies. For instance, regulations usually have sunset clauses, i.e. the regulations expire after a set period requiring them to be either allowed to lapse or be remade. A schedule for review or having an end date for policies is a good mechanism to ensure policies are regularly reviewed and that organisations are not caught out with their 'policy pants down'.

What Does Review of a Policy Entail?

There are two different types of policy review in my view:
- Formal Review.
- Evaluation.

Formal reviews take the least time to undertake and evaluation (which is a more comprehensive process) the most time. Which type of review is used for individual policies will depend on a number of factors:

- Risks of the policy.
- Complexity of the policy.
- Extent of changes in the external environment.
- Time and financial resources available for the review.

Conducting a Formal Review

As mentioned, a Formal Review is the quickest to do and least resource intensive. How comprehensive such a review is will depend on the factors detailed above. It may simply involve amending the policy to reflect any minor changes (titles, structure etc.) and then sending the policy to major stakeholders and subject matter experts for comment with a quick turnaround. Once this has been done the policy can go through the policy cycle starting at the consultation stage (see **Chapter 4**). Alternatively, a more comprehensive review may be required by following the complete policy cycle from the start.

Conducting an Evaluation

This is the best and preferred method of review but few organisations do it because it is resource intensive. It is suggested that this comprehensive method of review be undertaken where it involves complex issues, major risk areas, or major public policy areas (particularly where there is a large expenditure of money involved in the application of the policy).

It essentially involves testing the policy to determine whether it is in fact effective. Effective in the sense of whether it has achieved its purpose; if it has done what it was designed or intended to achieve. Is it working on the ground? That is, whether it is still good-policy (see **Introduction**).

I won't go into the details of conducting or commissioning an evaluation here as there are a number of methodologies available, depending on the type of policy and it's a specialist area. [47] However, broadly, the process involves:

- Testing the policy using an evaluative methodology. This ideally should be undertaken by someone who has expertise in policy evaluation and not be done by the policy developer.
- The policy developer then uses the outcomes of that evaluation to inform the policy development process which includes going through the complete policy cycle from the start.

Conclusion

As we have seen from this chapter the process of policy development is never completed. All stages of the policy cycle aim at developing good policy. But good policy is also policy that is being regularly reviewed to ensure it is doing what it was designed or intended to do because, after all, that's why the policy was developed in the first place. The review part of the policy cycle ensures that the policy that has been published remains good policy.

Scenario
Given the nature and importance of the issue, immigration policy, any issues identified on publication should be addressed immediately (as discussed above). Otherwise a Formal Review should take place at least a year after publication. Such a review should obtain the input of subject matter experts and all stakeholders (as previously identified) to assess whether the policy has addressed the issue that prompted development of the policy: clarifying the legislative requirements that apply to the assessment of applications by departmental officers. Evaluation may not be appropriate given the narrow nature of the policy unless it is part of a broader review of government immigration policy.

---

[47] Some sources of information on conducting evaluations are: Althous, Bridgman, and Davis (2018), pp.200ff; Argyrous (2010); Dye (2016); Bekkers, Fenger, and Scholten (2017), p.208ff.; Better Evaluation website (www.betterevaluation.org/en); Australian Evaluation Society website (www.aes.asn.au).

Chapter 7: Policy Development in a Nutshell

Good Policy

As we have seen, the policy cycle outlined in the previous chapters (**Chapters 2-6**) is all about supporting good policy development. Good policy, is effective policy, which is achieved by it being:

- On point – it addresses the issue or problem prompting the policy.
- Informed – it is well researched and consulted on.
- Comprehensive – it addresses all major issues and risks.
- Practical – it works in practice, "on the ground".
- Clear and accessible – it is easy to understand and to follow (from the audience or user perspective) and is readily available to users.

The Policy Cycle

In summary, and putting the policy cycle in the form of a checklist, the process to get to good policy is:

1. Determine the purpose of the proposed policy.
2. Research the policy subject and analyse that information.
3. Formulate the policy instrument.
4. Consult with key stakeholders on the policy instrument.
5. Obtain approval, publish and market the policy instrument.
6. Review, regularly, the policy instrument.

Throughout the policy cycle, the policy is progressively filled out. Initially, you start from a basic concept (the purpose of the policy) and end up with a policy instrument which provides the solution to the policy problem by comprehensively addressing specific issues and risks. Each stage of the policy cycle gives the policy greater focus, greater relevance, and more content.

Each stage in the cycle also supports and underpins the next. All stages of the policy cycle are equally important and inform the next stage. They are all interrelated. If you don't complete one stage of the policy cycle properly (e.g. you get the purpose wrong, don't research the policy subject thoroughly, or don't consult with the right people) then you will end up with bad policy.

Chapter 8: Beyond the Policy Cycle

Challenges & Threats to Good Policy

So far most of the book has been concerned with the process for the development of good policy. However, there is more to it than just following the policy cycle to get to good policy. It's not as simple as just following the policy development process to get to good policy.

There are a number of things that are required to support the policy process and to at least maximise the chances of developing good policy. A crucial one is that of policy capacity. Policy capacity comprises the skills and capabilities that are required to support the policy cycle. [48] Unless the policy cycle is supported by the necessary skills and capabilities, the process is effectively undermined. These skills and capabilities are required at the organisational and individual level. But even if there is policy capacity there are a number of other factors that can undermine good policy.

These are the issues I explore in this chapter.

Policy Capacity

Organisational Policy Capacity

At the organisational level, there are two core capabilities or requirements: [49]

- Support for the policy development function and process from senior management – the level of commitment to solving problems and evidence based policy development will impact on whether the policy cycle produces good policy.

---

[48] Wua, Ramesh and, Howlett (2015), p.166.
[49] Wua, Ramesh and, Howlett (2015), p.167.

- Adequacy of resources to support the policy development function – this includes financial support and the recruitment of personnel with the individual skills required (see below).

If you don't have enough money or sufficiently skilled people, you won't get good policy no matter how good the process.

Individual Policy Capacity

Introduction

As mentioned, there is a need for policy capacity at the individual level as well. The level of individual skill and capabilitity is a vital part of supporting the policy cycle. [50] Both those developing policies (policy developers) and those managing policy development processes (policy managers) need to have the right qualities and skills to support the process.

Policy Developers

Policy developers need to have a wide range of skills and capabilities:

Policy Development Skills

- Objectivity – this is probably the most important quality that a policy developer needs to have. Your own personal beliefs, opinions, and biases have no role to play in the policy development process. Policy development should be an objective process as far as is possible.
- Rationality – policy developers need to be able to think rationally and logically. This also means being perceptive. You need to have the ability to analyse and assess information; unpack problems; "join the dots"; develop solutions; and have an eye for detail. As mentioned, policy development is about problem solving, sometimes these are complex and difficult problems. [51]

---

[50] Wua, Ramesh and, Howlett (2015), p.167.
[51] Sparrow (2000) calls these "knotty problems". The term "wicked" problems has also been used in a policy context, see Katsonis (2019).

- Communication Skills – policy developers need excellent oral communication skills in order to consult and liaise with supervisors, managers, subject matter experts, stakeholders etc. They also need excellent written skills, as they need to be able to write clear and comprehensive policy instruments using Plain English principles.
- Consultation Skills – one of the most important things a policy developer needs to have is the ability to consult. This goes beyond communications skills. They need to know when to consult and with whom (i.e. have organisational knowledge). In particular they need to be aware of the need to regularly consult with the policy manager during the policy development process. Keeping the policy manager up to date of where they are at in relation to the development of the policy from start to finish is vital (and by this I don't mean hourly or daily updates). Most policy developers need to understand when to seek advice and assistance from policy managers (that usually means a lot of times). Consultation also includes using colleagues to bounce ideas off. Consulting with the policy manager is not only necessary so that they know where things are at (in case they are asked by their management) but it is to protect the policy developer from going off on a tangent or getting into trouble by doing something inappropriate (particularly when seeking advice or assistance outside the organisation).
- Organisational Skills – policy developers need to be well organised. Organised and structured in the approach to developing policy and also in keeping good records. Through the whole policy cycle, policy developers need to keep some sort of file or record that contains absolutely everything associated with development of the policy (in chronological order). Nothing should be thrown away. Notes should be kept (whether electronic or on paper) of what has been done in

relation to the policy, so it is clear what has been done and what stage the policy is at. Everything needs to be documented. Policy development has a high degree of accountability and good records are vital to address any issues raised by someone with the content of the policy or the process in developing it. This is a self-protection measure for the policy developer, apart from protecting the integrity of the process.

Knowledge of the Policy Development Process

Policy developers need to understand how the policy development process works in practice and its various components. In particular, they should have an understanding of the rationale that underpins every part of the policy cycle. They also should keep up to date with policy trends and research. Excellent website sources are: APO Analysis and Policy Observatory; [52] The Mandarin. [53] and Alliance for Useful Evidence. [54] There are also a number of useful journals, such as *Evidence & Policy* [55] and *Law & Policy*. [56]

Personal Qualities

- Integrity & Accountability – policy developers need to have a high degree of integrity. By this I mean policy developers need to be open and honest. Hand in hand with integrity is accountability. Policy developers must prepare themselves for criticism when consulting on the policy and, more so, when it is actually published. The whole process of policy development often results in compromise, making choices in relation to ideas and issues, or in the killing off of hobby horses. That means, sometimes "offending" people. Rarely do policy developers get congratulations for producing a good policy (particularly from those subject to the policy).

---

[52] https://apo.org.au/
[53] www.themandarin.com.au/
[54] https://www.alliance4usefulevidence.org/
[55] https://policy.bristoluniversitypress.co.uk/journals/evidence-and-policy
[56] https://onlinelibrary.wiley.com/journal/14679930.

That's the nature of the job. Policy developers are stuck between management (who have one view of what the policy should contain) and those subject to the policy who have a different view (and who sometimes believe there is no need for the policy at all). However, if the policy has properly gone through the policy cycle and it has been documented (see above) then policy developers are in a position to defend the policy, their work and integrity. But remember the policy environment is constantly changing and things can go wrong. Policy developers should accept that and move on, never take it personally.

- Empathy – policy development is a people orientated job. Policy developers are constantly dealing with a variety of people and personalities: managers, team members, subject matter experts, stakeholders, and those subject to policies. Therefore, policy developers need to be able to get on with and understand people. There is no room for prickly or grumpy personalities.

Policy Managers

Those that manage policy development processes (policy managers) also play a vital role in ensuring the process leads to good policy. Often whether a policy is a good or bad one comes down to decisions made by managers during a policy's development. As well as the same requirements a policy developers, managers should also have the following skills and attributes:

Management Skills

- Team Development – policy managers usually have more experience in policy development than most team members (if they don't they are at a significant disadvantage). Therefore, they have a duty to pass on that experience. One of the main roles of a manager is to develop staff so that they can acquire skills, and frankly, succeed you. The manager won't be there forever. No point on holding onto knowledge as if it was a precious metal. If a policy manager invests in the team, they will develop their skills, do a better job, be happier in the job, and the policy manager will have less work to do as they will become more autonomous. The policy manager carries the can for the work team members produce. A golden rule is to never sell team members down the river. If it is a performance issue, that is something that needs to be addressed individually and confidentially.

- Delegation of Responsibility – linked to the above point, is that policy managers should have the ability to delegate work and tasks (subject to appropriate supervision) to staff. Skills in staff are developed by delegation and honed by appropriate oversight. There is nothing worse than a policy manager that tries to do everything themselves or is constantly peering over the shoulder of staff to see what they are up to. I think they call this micro-managing.

- Development of an Open and Collaborative Environment – policy development (and the development of staff) is best achieved in an environment in which there is open communication and collaboration amongst team members. Policy managers should make it clear to team members that they can ask you anything, anytime (even if it is critical of you). You should listen and welcome input. Team members should also be encouraged to help each other, to share knowledge, different points of view, to challenge ideas etc. [57] However, this needs to be done in a supportive and respectful environment with the policy manager being the "referee" if needed. To support this, managers should hold regular meetings individually with staff to monitor their progress and to give them

---

[57] In relation to an approach for the testing and challenging of ideas, I particularly favour the Socratic method which "...is a form of cooperative argumentative dialogue between individuals, based on asking and answering questions to stimulate critical thinking and to draw out ideas and underlying presuppositions." (Wikipedia).

any assistance or advice. Also they should hold regular team meetings then the whole team know who is working on what. In this way, other team member's expertise can be accessed and shared, at the meeting or one on one.

- Administrative & Human Resource Skills – an obvious requirement is for a policy manager to have the appropriate administrative skills to support staff to do their job. In particular dealing with the numerous human resource issues that arise in managing the team. Such tasks are the responsibility of the manager not staff. Staff should be free to do get on with developing policies!

- Good Judgment – this is simply "...the ability to the combine personal qualities with relevant knowledge and experience to form opinions and make decisions." [58] In a policy context, particularly, good judgement is required to make the call on policy direction and priorities.

Policy Skills

- Appropriate Assignment of Policy Development Tasks – Policy managers should understand the need to assign policy tasks to team members on the basis of skills, expertise or aptitude. If they don't have an area of expertise, this can be developed by assigning them policy development tasks on a specific subject. That gives team members confidence and develops their skills and competence. When assigning specific policy development tasks, policy managers should make sure that the paperwork (file or brief) gives sufficient information to assist the team member to commence the task (particularly in regard to the purpose and scope of the policy development task). If this information is not there, provide it on the file, or if you are aware of other issues, also note this on the file.

---

[58] Likierman (2020). This article goes in more detail on what are the elements of good judgment.

- Quality Control – policy managers need to ensure quality control of the product coming out of the policy area. All policy instruments from formulation to the publication stages of the policy cycle should be reviewed by the policy manager before they go out of the policy area. This is to ensure quality control, then the policy manager knows where each policy is at, and more importantly that that the policy cycle has been followed properly. However, policy managers should never rewrite a policy instrument for a team member. Only comments and suggestions should be provided. Don't be so hands on so that your "…paw prints are evident on every word." [59] Staff will never learn anything if the policy manager does their work for them. It doesn't matter how many times a policy has to be redrafted, do not be tempted! Believe me this is the best way for team members to develop their policy development skills!

Political Acumen

Political knowledge and experience is an important skill but more so in relation to higher level policy issues.[60] Identifying the key stakeholders and understanding their interests, motivations, and views, as well as an understanding of the trade-offs necessary for agreement or consensus among conflicting interests is also important. Policy managers need to be able to understand what their stakeholders and senior managers want and need in order to "sell" proposed policies.

Factors Undermining Good Policy

Introduction

I have written this book as if the policy development process is a pure process that is not affected by any external factors; that policy

---

[59] Cutts (1995), p. 124.
[60] Wua, Ramesh and, Howlett (2015), p.169.

developers and policy managers have complete control over the process and the content of the policy. Of course, this is not reality. There
is more to it than just following the bouncing policy cycle ball. There
are several external factors that sometimes work against good policy:

- Politics
- Quality of Evidence
- Time

Politics

Politics is potentially the major obstacle to good policy. Politics
is '...the way in which societies deal with the balancing and alloca-
tion of values that is necessary to deal with challenges that a society
as a political community is confronted with." [61]

In the context of public policy this means the content and direction of policies is subject to influence by government priorities, its
policy agenda, or interest groups to whom the government listens.
After all this is what, at least high level, public policy is all about,
right? As the Institute of Public Administration Australia has ob-
served: [62]

> Within the contemporary policymaking environment, with its diverse
> constituencies, stakeholders, and access points, there is pressure for
> senior politicians in governments and oppositions to make decisions
> quickly and confidently in order to appear decisive, pander to populist
> ideas to appear responsive, manufacture wedge issues to distinguish
> themselves from their opponents, and to put a spin on everything to
> exaggerate its significance. At other times some leaders like to be seen
> to be making up their own minds, rather than following a course of
> action being advocated by somebody else (irrespective of the merits).

Politics is part of the process and ultimately the government
"owns" public policy, it has the final say on the content of such policy. However, it does not always play a positive role and doesn't
always support good policy. In a public policy context, politicians

---

[61] Bekkers, Fenger, and Scholten (2017), p. 6.
[62] Institute of Public Administration Australia (2012), p. vi.

sometimes argue that as they are the ones that are elected they have the authority and responsibility to make the policy decisions. That is true, the buck stops with them (or at least it should). However, it does not mean every policy decision they make is not impacted by subjective factors. Factors that undermine good policy.

The influence of politics may be seen at the start of the cycle (by determining the purpose of the policy (or throughout the rest of the cycle). There may be pressure for policy to reflect government priorities and policy. Therefore, political priorities and influence might distort the outcomes of the policy development process. In this way politics has the potential to undermine good policy.

Politics can also play a role in other areas of policy, such as operational policy, where the direction and content of policy may be influenced by the priorities and views of the organisation's management rather than outcomes obtained through the application of the policy cycle.

When subjective political elements are introduced into the policy development process, good policy can be undermined.

Quality of Evidence

Linked to the challenges politics poses to good policy, the amount and quality of information available on any given policy subject challenges good policy. There is a plethora of information on any given subject. Anyone can say and publish anything they like on the Internet, more often than not reflecting their own personal agendas and ideologies. Some of these views are often disguised as research and expertise. It is a challenge to evidence based policy. In this environment it is sometimes hard to tell what is evidence, as Gary Banks has stated: [63]

> "...evidence-based policy making faces the challenge that this thing we call 'evidence' is rarely the uncontested and objective policy resource that we might imagine it to be. Rather, it can be a battleground

---

[63] Gary Banks (2018), p.5.

of conflicting views, assumptions and interpretations. And therefore the notion that 'evidence' should win the day in its own right, appealing as it may be to the research and evaluation community, is fanciful."

Time

The time available to develop a policy is a major factor in whether the process produces good policy. The more complex the policy, the more time you need as a policy developer. However, for various reasons (political, financial, workload, risk) you may not always get the time. That means compromising on some aspects of the policy cycle which may impact on whether the process produces good policy or not.

The complexity of the policy issue and associated risks (political, economic, financial, human, and/or reputational) should be the prime determiners of the time allocated to development of the policy. As a policy developer you are in a good position to understand the complexity and risks, and therefore advocate for the appropriate time to be allocated for policy development. But sometimes it's out of your control and you need to just suck it in.

Conclusion

Good process can lead to good policy but it does not guarantee it. There are two major factors which can affect whether following the policy cycle results in good policy.

First, the policy process must be supported at both the organisational and individual level. There must be policy capacity. That is, at the organisational level there must be support for the policy development function and process as well as the resources to support it. At the individual level, policy developers and policy managers must have the qualities and skills to properly support the policy development process.

Secondly there are a number of external factors, such as politics, quality of evidence, and time, that can undermine good policy.

Policy developers, and their managers, need to be aware of these factors which may undermine their efforts in striving to produce good policy. However, the nature of policy development is that sometimes little can be done to combat, at least some of, these factors – particularly the external factors, no matter what you do. In this case you try to get to as close as possible to good policy as possible. But the reality is that good policy is an ideal, not often achieved, but that's not a reason why not to aim for it. When developing a policy your aim should be the ideal and if you fall short, due to factors outside your control, that is the nature of the policy development task with all its variables. But we never improve if we don't have an objective, an ideal, something to aim for. By striving for the ideal we incrementally improve the standard of policy development and the status of the policy development function. Policy development is never about the acceptance of the status quo. But you need an ideal, a target, and the policy cycle provides the framework to aim for this.

In summary, following the policy cycle does not guarantee good policy because of the complexity of policy development including the factors that work against good policy. However, that does not undermine the legitimacy and efficacy of the policy cycle. The policy cycle is still the best blueprint we have for developing good policy. The factors that work against the process do not undermine or devalue its basic aim, which is getting to good policy. That's the nature of policy development. Nor does it undermine its value or utility.

However, we have to remember that policy development is in itself a complex task. As I said previously it is more an art than a science. It is more than just a process: [64]

> Policy making is fundamentally a problem-solving and creative activity. It is not easily amenable to a menu or 'cookbook' approach. It involves the application of knowledge and thinking – deductively

---

[64] Institute of Public Administration Australia (2012), p. 4.

(around cause-effect relationships) or inductively (looking for patterns and trends).

References

Althaus, Catherine; Bridgman, Peter; and Davis, Glyn (2018) *The Australian Policy Handbook*, 6th Edition, Crows Nest, Allen & Unwin.

Andrews, Matt (2018) 'Public Policy Failure: 'How Often" and 'What is Failure, Anyway'? Center for International Development (Harvard University) Working Paper No. 344 (https://bsc.cid.harvard.edu/publications/public-policy-failure(,

Argyrous, George (editor) (2010) *Evidence for Policy and Decision Making*, Sydney, University of New South Wales Press.

Baldwin, Robert and Cave, Martin (1999) *Understanding Regulation*, New York, Oxford University Press.

Banks, Gary (2018) 'Whatever Happened to 'Evidence Based Policy Making'?', Alf Rattigan Lecture 2018, Australia & New Zealand School of Government (https://www.anzsog.edu.au/preview-documents/research-output/5307-alf-rattigan-lecture-2018/file).

Bekkers, Victor; Fenger, Menno, and Scholten, Peter (2017), *Public Policy in Action*, Cheltenham UK, Edward Elgar Publishing.

Cairney, Paul (2012) *Understanding Public Policy*, Houndmills, Basingstoke, Palgrave Macmillan.

Campbell, Nancy J. (1997) *Writing Effective Policies and Procedures*, New York, Amacom.

Centre for Public Impact (2018) *A brief introduction to... Human-centred design and behavioural science* (https://resources.centreforpublicimpact.org/production/2018/08/CPI-A-brief-introduction-to...-Human-centred-design.pdf).

Cutts, Martin (1995) *The Plain English Guide*, Oxford, Oxford University Press.

Cutts, Martin (2013) *Oxford Guide to Plain English*, Oxford, Oxford University Press.

Daddow, Oliver (2019) *Police Success and Failure: Embedding Effective Learning in Government*, Bennett Institute for Public Policy (www.bennettinstitute.cam.ac.uk/publications/policy-success-and-failure)

Dye, Thomas R. (2016) *Understanding Public Policy*, 15th Edition, New York, Pearson.

Einfeld, Colette (2019) 'Nudge and Evidence Based Policy: Fertile Ground', *Evidence & Policy*, 15(4) November 2019, pp 509-524,

Frieberg, Arie (2017) *Regulation in Australia*, Sydney, The Federation Press.

Howlett, Michael (2014) 'Policy Design: What, How and Why?', in Halpers, Charlotte, Lascoumes, Pierre, and Le Galès, Patrick (2014) L'instrumentation et ses effets, Paris, Presses de Sciencies Po.

Hudson, Bob (2019) 'We Need to Talk About Policy Failure – and how to avoid it' *Apolotical* (https://apolitical.co/solution_article/how-to-avoid-policy-failure/

Institute of Public Administration Australia (2012) *Public Policy Drift*: www.ipaa.org.au/wp-content/uploads/2019/06/Public-Policy-Drift-policy-paper.pdf.

Katsonis, Maria (2019), 'What's so wicked about wicked problems?', *The Mandarin,* May 13, 2019 (https://www.themandarin.com.au/108345-wicked-problem/)

Lesh, Matthew (2019) *Evidence Based Policy Research Project, 20 Case Studies*, Institute of Public Affairs, November 2019 (https://ipa.org.au/wp-content/uploads/2019/11/Evidence-Based-Policy-Research-Project-20-Case-Studies.pdf)

Likierman, Andrew Sir (2020), 'The Elements of Good Judgment', *Harvard Business Review*, January-February 2020 (https://hbr.org/2020/01/the-elements-of-good-judgment)

Lipsky, Michael. (1980) *Street-level Bureaucracy: dilemmas of the individual in public services*, New York, Russell Sage Foundation.

Macdonald, Ros and Clark-Dickson, Deborah (2010) *Clear and Precise: Writing Skills for Today's Lawyers*, Pyrmont, New South Wales, Thomson Reuters.

Macquarie Dictionary (2017), Seventh Edition, Sydney, Macquarie Dictionary Publishers.

Moilanen, Stephen (2019) 'When to Use User-Centered Design for Public Policy', *Stanford Social Innovation Review* (https://ssir.org/articles/entry/when_to_use_user_centered_design_for_public_policy#)

Ogrizek, Mick (2018) *Australian Childcare Regulation*, Bright Victoria, Mick Ogrizek. (available only through www.lulu.com).

Page, Stephen (2000) *Achieving 100% Compliance of Policies and Procedures*, Mansfield Ohio, Bookmasters Inc.

Per Capita (2019), *Evidence Based Policy Analysis: 20 Case Studies* (https://percapita.org.au/our_work/evidence-based-policy-analysis-2019)

Savage, Chas (2019) 'Writing: Five Ways to Get Your Brief Read by the Minister', *The Mandarin* (www.themandarin.com.au/2220-communications-five-ways-get-brief-read-ministers/).

Sparrow, Malcolm K (2000) *The Regulatory Craft: Controlling Risks, Solving Problems, and Managing Compliance*, Washington DC, Brookings Institution Press.

Style Manual (2002), Sixth Edition, Canberra, John Wiley & Sons Australia Ltd.

Thaler, Richard H. and Sunstein, Cass R. (2009) *Nudge*, London, Penguin Books.

UK Policy Profession Board (2013), *Twelve Actions to Professionalise Policy Making*.
(https://civilservicelearning.civilservice.gov.uk/sites/default/files/twelve_actions_report_web_accessible.pdf)

Victorian Government (2016), *Victorian Guide to Regulation* (www.dtf.vic.gov.au/funds-programs-and-policies/victorian-guide-regulation).

Wua, X, Ramesh, M and Howlett, M (2015), 'Policy Capacity: a Conceptual Framework for Understanding Policy Competences and Capabilities', *Policy and Society* 34 (2015) 165–171.

www.ingramcontent.com/pod-product-compliance
Lightning Source LLC
Chambersburg PA
CBHW070259290526
45791CB00003B/1013